THE
UNPLUGGING

Also by Yvette Nolan

Annie Mae's Movement
Medicine Shows: Indigenous Performance Culture
Performing Indigeneity (edited with Ric Knowles)
Refractions: Scenes (edited with Donna-Michelle St. Bernard)
Refractions: Solo (edited with Donna-Michelle St. Bernard)

THE
UNPLUGGING

YVETTE NOLAN

PLAYWRIGHTS CANADA PRESS

TORONTO

LIBRARY AND ARCHIVES CANADA CATALOGUING IN PUBLICATION
Nolan, Yvette
    The unplugging / Yvette Nolan.

Issued also in electronic format.
ISBN 978-1-77091-132-1

    I. Title.

PS8577.O426U67 2013   C812'.54   C2012-907939-1

Playwrights Canada Press operates on Mississaugas of the Credit, Wendat, Anishinaabe, Métis, and Haudenosaunee land. It always was and always will be Indigenous land.

We acknowledge the financial support of the Canada Council for the Arts, the Ontario Arts Council (OAC), Ontario Creates, and the Government of Canada for our publishing activities.

for Kugler who gave me the story
Donna who gave me the deadline
Randy who gave me the reason
and Philip who gave me the space

If Yvette Nolan is a bit of a seer, a fortuneteller, as I suspect she and many writers are, our society is cruising toward an unplugging of our own. Halfway into this play in your hands, the character Bernadette speaks of natural disasters. She claims that she foresaw the eponymous "unplugging," a term she invents to describe the sudden termination of all the technology in their world: "I used to think of it as the earth waking and shaking like some great dog, and all the machines and wires being shaken off like so many fleas. The earthquakes in Haiti and Japan, the disappearance of the Maldives... But that was really negative. The unplugging is more—benign." She paints a vivid picture of the chaos that ensued, and, chillingly, admits that despite sensing its arrival, she didn't prepare for the unplugging. This strikes an uneasy chord, articulating that unspoken, creeping feeling of disquiet with our own digital dependence. Just during the rehearsals and premiere run of this play, we saw major earthquakes on the West Coast in the Haida Gwaii region, and Hurricane Sandy in the Caribbean and along the US East Coast, forcing closed the New York Stock Exchange, flooding the subway system, and plunging Manhattan into the dark, unplugging millions.

Yvette is an astute observer of the everyday and of the larger global movements that form and inform our lives and politics. *The Unplugging* speaks to both ends of that spectrum, the small, domestic negotiations between people and the vast landscape of our negotiations with Nature. A negotiation we seem to be losing right now. She prompts us to think about our relationship to the land, our relationship to knowledge and how we acquire it and to the construction and nurturing of community.

It's an urgent prompt, but she isn't reproving us. She's posing a genuine question about our future to artists and audiences. Bernadette, Elena and Seamus are like us—just as smart and savvy and stranded, as many of us would be in a global—or domestic—crisis.

In the spirit of the play and its strong case for sharing knowledge freely, I'm going to pass on some things I learned about the play during rehearsals. The non-verbal life in this story is as important as the spoken text. The passage of time between scenes is a gift to a director and her team. Explore them as you would a scene. The spare stage directions for these transitions are an invitation for the creative team (and reader) to invent the physical and visual world of the play. Everything can be mined: unspoken conversations between characters, the presence of nature, the labour of surviving, even the specific relationships the characters have with objects—a favourite knife, a faulty zipper, a misplaced... etc. All this is fruitful territory to explore in rehearsals; give it the time and space to breathe and you will create a credible and rich world for these characters to inhabit.

Writers, in my experience, are very deliberate about their work. There isn't a word in this play that Yvette hasn't considered. Enter this universe with an open mind, and when confronted with contradictions, embrace them. The emotional complexity of the characters lies in this reconciling. There's action and story in the white space on the page. Listen closely and you will hear Yvette as if she is sitting right next to you—her unique rhythms, her sly humour, her generous politics.

—Rachel Ditor, Literary Manager, Arts Club Theatre Company

An excerpt of this play, originally titled *Two Old Women*, was read at Native Earth Performing Arts's Weesageechak Begins to Dance XXII on January 28, 2010, under the direction of Randy Reinholz, with performances by Maev Beatty, Patti Shaughnessy and James Cade.

The play underwent a further workshop at the Playwrights Theatre Centre in Vancouver in April 2010, once again under the direction of Randy Reinholz, with performances by Margo Kane, Marie Clements and Troy Kozuki.

In June 2010, the playwright was a member of the Banff Playwrights Colony. *Two Old Women* was read there by Val Pearson, Elinor Holt and Stafford Perry under the direction of Rachel Ditor.

In October 2010, *Two Old Women* was read at the Arts Club Theatre ReACT festival, once again under the direction of Rachel Ditor, with Margo Kane, Marie Clements and Charlie Gallant.

The play was read at the University of Toronto's Festival of Original Theatre on February 4, 2011, with performances by Tara Beagan, Michaela Washburn and James Cade.

The play received public readings at the Matariki Festival in Wellington, New Zealand, on June 26, 2010, and at Reverie Productions in New York City on June 29, 2011.

Ongoing dramaturgy has been provided by DD Kugler and Rachel Ditor.

The Unplugging premiered at the Arts Club Theatre (Artistic Director Bill Millerd) on the Revue Stage in Vancouver, Canada, on October 17, 2012, with the following company:

Elena: Margo Kane
Bern: Jenn Griffin
Seamus: Anton Lipovetsky

Director: Lois Anderson
Set designer: Drew Facey
Costume designer: Vanessa Imeson
Lighting designer: Jeff Harrison
Sound designer: Alison Jenkins
Dramaturg: Rachel Ditor
Stage manager: Pamela Jakobs
Apprentice stage manager: Stephanie Meine

CHARACTERS

Elena
Bern
Seamus

NOTE ON THE PUNCTUATION

I have tried to capture the way people actually talk, in bits and pieces, generally with fewer full stops, and less complete thoughts. Conversation like a badminton game, keeping the birdie in the air.

part of you pours out of me
in these lines from time to time
—Joni Mitchell

BANISHED

Moon. Cold. Silver light. The sound of footsteps on snow. The snow squeaks with the footsteps, the way it does when it is so cold. But a dry cold. Two women walk on. BERN *is carrying a large pack and dragging a child's wooden toboggan, laden with sleeping bags, a tarp, other accumulated supplies.* ELENA *is carrying nothing. Both are wearing parkas, big boots. Halfway across,* ELENA *sits in the snow.* BERN *keeps walking off. A moment of* ELENA *sitting, stupefied.*

BERN   Elena?

BERN rushes back on.

Elena. Are you hurt?

ELENA just sits.

Ah. Just your feelings. Come on. Get up. You will freeze to death sitting here. And I will freeze to death standing over you trying to convince you to get up and move. Come on. Elena. Come on.

I can't start a fire here. It's too open, too windy. Even if I could find enough wood. Come on, we're close now.

ELENA   they say freezing to death is nice.

BERN   sure they do.

ELENA   they say you just get sleepy, then slip away

BERN   what they? Who is this they?

ELENA   common wisdom

BERN   common wisdom. They probably just say that to comfort family members who cannot bear the thought of their people suffering.

ELENA   they say—

BERN   For godssake, Elena, I'm from Winnipeg and you're from Saskatoon. We've both come pretty close to freezing. How nice is that memory?

ELENA   They say bleeding to death is very nice.

BERN   Oh yeah, exsanguination is great. I almost bled to death the last time I miscarried. It was great. *That's* when you get very sleepy. Come on. Get up… Besides, if you opened a vein here it would probably freeze over in seconds.

ELENA   Bernadette, just leave me. I don't want to go on.

BERN   I don't want to go on. How very—dramatic—of you. We must go on.

ELENA   you go on.

BERN   I am not going on without you.

ELENA   you say that.

BERN   I mean it.

ELENA   It's okay, Bernadette. You don't have to take care of me. You'll do better by yourself.

BERN   I am not abandoning you. Besides. I don't think that's true.

ELENA   what?

BERN   that I will do better by myself. I need you, Elena.

ELENA   me? A useless old dried-up—

BERN   stop. Stop that.

ELENA   That's why we are out here, isn't it? Exiled? Because we are old.

BERN   We are not old.

ELENA   that's what they said

BERN   Yes, well. Times have changed. Fifty is the new eighty, I guess.

ELENA   This is not how I thought it would end.

BERN   It's not over. We're not over.

ELENA   Well, you're a pushy broad so I guess it's not over for me yet.
But the world. It's not looking good for the world.

BERN   Some say the world will end in fire,
Some say in ice.
From what I've tasted of desire
I hold with those who favor fire.
But if it had to perish twice,
I think I know enough of hate
To say that for destruction ice
Is also great
And would suffice.

ELENA   nice

BERN   funny.

ELENA   *(beat)* Did you just make that up?

BERN   I wish. A man named Frost.

ELENA   ha.

BERN   ha.

ELENA   I guess he's dead now.

BERN   oh yes, he's been dead—oh—fifty years

ELENA   oh. Lucky him.

BERN   Elena.

ELENA   probably died in his bed surrounded by his *family*

BERN   Elena.

ELENA   in his warm, clean bed, surrounded by his family who were sad to see him go, tears streaming down their faces… he probably died of old age, not banished from his community, driven out like a dog

BERN   there were tears streaming down your daughter's face

ELENA   pft

BERN   and Archer's

ELENA   he's a good boy

BERN   he *is* a good boy.

he left us this

She reaches into her pack and pulls out a hatchet.

ELENA   a hatchet?

BERN   his hatchet

ELENA   Bernadette, the world is full of hatchets. Hatchets and knives and guns and tons of useless dead things. Dead cars, dead stereos, dead computers, dead telephones, dead rockets, dead dead dead.

BERN   It's the thought that counts.

ELENA   I suppose.

BERN   and the world may be full of hatchets, but—they may not be as easy to put your hands on as they once were. Can't really stroll into the Canadian Tire and browse in the camping section.

ELENA   No. I guess not. Anything that useful must be long gone.

BERN   So it's a fine gift.

ELENA   It is a fine gift.

BERN   Come on. I think we're close.

ELENA   Close to what? There is no house. Who would live up here? Mad trappers and renegades.

BERN   Yup, and old hippies and back-to-the-landers and apocalyptists.

ELENA   Nice company you keep.

BERN   lucky for us. Come on, Elena. This is all starting to look familiar—

ELENA   oh my bones.

BERN   Elena.

ELENA   what. Fine. I am coming.

SURVIVAL

Inside the log house. BERN *tends a simple, old airtight wood stove. It might be a top-loader. It has no glass, no way to watch the fire within, its primary function to heat the house quickly.* ELENA *just sits.*

BERN he built it before they ran the power in up here. Way easier to heat, light and ventilate than to try and adapt something that was never intended to be without electricity

> BERN *pours a cup of tea and takes it to* ELENA.

bless the last hiker or hunter or whoever left tea

ELENA probably kill me

BERN I don't think tea goes bad… I don't recall ever hearing of any-one dying of tea that had gone off

> BERN *pours herself a cup and smells it.*

smells okay. Woodsy. I wonder if that is normal.

ELENA   google it

BERN   ha.

ELENA   think of all the information that disappeared, in a blink. All the things we stopped writing down and putting in books, all the things we stopped teaching our children, all the things we need to know now, like, what is the shelf life of tea, and if it passes its best-before date, can it kill you. I hope so.

> *ELENA drinks.*

> *BERN continues to caretake, bringing in wood, tending the fire, putting a pot of snow on the wood stove maybe, enumerating a meagre pile of supplies: the hatchet, a lighter that still works, a couple of cans of vegetables, a package of noodles, a half box of salt, a roll of toilet paper, a box of wooden matches. She smells the matches to see if they are dry and still usable. She examines the cans for bulges or leaks, best-before dates. ELENA sits and drinks tea.*

    it's going to be dark soon

BERN   oh, you're still with us, are you?

ELENA   you haven't touched yours

BERN   Elena, I'm *working*.

ELENA   Sit for a second. Relax.

BERN   Relax? *Relax?* I can't *relax*, Elena. It will be dark soon. I haven't found any candles or lamps or any way to make light. I don't know if there's someone out there who also thinks this house makes a great shelter, and doesn't care that we were here first, because he's bigger and stronger than I am. We don't have anything to eat, not really, and it's December, it's *December*, Elena, at least I think it's December, which means there are five or six months before we can grow anything, or harvest anything. I need you, Elena, I need you to help. I can't do it all anymore, I can't do all the scrounging and the encouraging and the planning and the hoping.

> *ELENA nods. She gets out of her chair, goes to* BERN, *indicates she should sit.* BERN *sits.* ELENA *goes to retrieve* BERN's *tea, carries it to her where she sits.*

ELENA   You should drink it now. While it still has some warmth in it. Plus you haven't had enough water today. You'll get dehydrated.

> BERN *takes her tea, smells it. She is unconvinced.*

It's fine, Bernadette. *(beat)* That woodsy smell is just stale-ness. Happens after four or five years. But there's no mould. Whoever left it sealed it well.

> BERN *drinks.*

BERN   Ahhh.

ELENA   See? Not bad.

> *They sit.* BERN *drinks her tea.* ELENA *watches her. After a bit,* ELENA *goes and gets the pot, refills* BERN's *cup.*

BERN   Elena, I— *(She goes to get up.)*

ELENA   Sit. Drink your tea.

> ELENA *checks the pot to see how much is left. She pours out the last few drops into her cup, downs it. Then she goes out.*

BERN drinks her tea. She cries, not hysterically, but almost as if she does not know she is crying.

ELENA comes back carrying a lantern.

let there be light

BERN   where did you get that?

ELENA   outhouse.

She shakes the lantern.

there's probably enough in there for tonight, and then we will figure out what to burn in it.

BERN   ever smart, you

ELENA   and—

She pulls a candle out of her pocket.

BERN   wow.

ELENA   whoever's place it was did not like to do his business in the dark

BERN   lucky for us. *(beat)* How'd you know that about the tea?

ELENA   what about the tea?

BERN   that it smells woodsy when it gets old

ELENA   my grandma, I guess. She never really trusted the technology. Never used a bank card. Drove an ancient truck with a standard transmission. Fixed things instead of throwing them out.

BERN   I never knew my grandparents. I wish I had. So much I don't know about where I come from.

ELENA   It was an accident really. My mother used to send me to my father in the summers. He'd pick me up at the bus station near his community, take me to his place, not much more than a shack really. He'd last a couple of days, trying to be a dad, to care about my life… then he'd vanish.

BERN   Like—disappear?

ELENA   well, there'd be a note—"Have to go work"—and I wouldn't see him again.

BERN   He wasn't able to be a parent.

ELENA   Oh no. I have no idea how he got together with my mother in the first place. He probably left the marriage the same way—"Have to go work."

BERN   how old were you? When he left you in the shack?

ELENA   the first time? Maybe seven.

BERN   He left a seven-year-old alone?

       ELENA laughs.

ELENA   After he'd been gone a couple of days, my grandma would show up. I don't know how she knew. And we'd go out on the land. Check her traps, hunt, pick medicines.

BERN   lucky for us

ELENA   When she got really old, she was tiny, like a bird, they put her
        in a home, but she wouldn't stay. She kept running away. Died
        in the bush.

        That's what they did to us, Bern.

BERN   They didn't lock us up, Elena.

ELENA   no, they pushed us out. They drove us out.

BERN   they used to do that. Before.

ELENA   They?

BERN   We used to do that. People. In tough times—we—used to leave
        people behind.

ELENA   because we were a nomadic people! we haven't lived like that
        in centuries.

BERN   still

ELENA   Our community—our so-called community—did not leave
        us behind. It is still there, building walls and gathering up guns
        to point at whoever they don't want inside the walls.

BERN   *(beat)* not much of a community.

ELENA   *(beat)* not much of a community

        There is a long, full silence.

        Sun is going. Good time to see if this thing will actually work.

BERN   It's not quite dark yet. Don't you think we should save it—

ELENA   you say there's other cabins around here

BERN   yeah, it's quite the village. Was.

ELENA   well, tomorrow you will begin to check those other places for more fuel. All these back-to-the-landers, someone is bound to have a supply—

> *She fusses with the lantern, then puts a match to the wick. It casts a warm oil-fed light.*

BERN   and there was light

ELENA   And god saw the light, that it was good.

BERN   I don't think god has anything to do with it, Elena. God tiptoed from the world when everyone was looking elsewhere.

> *They sit looking at the light, the flame and each other.*

NEW YEAR

Time passes, moving from Little Spirit Moon, December, to Spirit Moon, January. The passage of time can be indicated by movement and light, by the characters building routines, by accumulating things, by building the space in which they live together.

LOVE

BERN comes in with a load of wood.

BERN   oh my god, what is that smell?

ELENA   that is pebeepebonbon—rabbit stew

BERN   rabbit. Stew.

ELENA   well, stew might be a little generous. Since it is mostly rabbit. But I found some carrots and some onion up at the monk's place.

BERN   I don't know why you insist on calling that the monk's place.

ELENA   it pleases me to think of him as a monk. Living up there alone, next to the creek, communing with nature. His house is built like a temple to nature. Open spaces, windows that let the sun shine in, simple, elegant, functional. I like to imagine him sitting there, meditating. A Franciscan monk—

BERN   so the monk managed to keep carrots?

ELENA under his floor, in sand. Cold but not frozen.

BERN really

ELENA smart monk. People often just left vegetables like carrots in the garden and covered the row with straw or hay, harvest them as they need them. if he did that though, they'd be long gone, so it's good for us that he knew that sand trick. You know, the monk's place might make a good greenhouse, all that glass in that corner where he meditated—

BERN lifts the lid on the pot.

BERN rabbit.

ELENA takes the lid and puts it back on the pot.

ELENA he was a good size too. You know, Bern, if you could find a gun—

BERN I'm looking, Elena. Every place, I check for a gun. Though I'm not sure I really want to find a gun.

ELENA If I had a rifle though, I could take a deer. Or a moose. A moose would mean meat for the winter, not having to check dozens of traps in the hope of catching one or two skinny hares.

BERN don't denigrate the poor skinny hare. It was generous of him to step into your little noose—

ELENA *Snare.* Yes. But if we got a moose, Bern, we could make jerky, and stew, and the hide would be useful for—

BERN shakes her head in wonder.

what? I could take a moose.

BERN   I have no doubt that you could, Elena.

ELENA   then what?

BERN   Back there, I never would have guessed that you were this person—so capable, so—

ELENA   I wasn't this person back there. They were right to expel me. I *was* a burden. I was negative and bitchy and—you know what they called me?

BERN   Eeyore.

ELENA   you knew?

BERN   everyone knew.

ELENA   you know who Eeyore was?

BERN   of course

ELENA   I had to look it up. In a book. Took me ages 'cause I couldn't figure out how to spell Eeyore. And I had no idea what I was looking for. How do you look for something you don't know?

BERN   you never read *Winnie-the-Pooh*?

ELENA   Well, if I had I wouldn't have had to look it up, would I? I had to go to the library. It was creepy. Libraries were creepy when they were—before—now that they're abandoned, they're even worse.

BERN   I love libraries. Loved. Full of other peoples' lives, full of other peoples' thoughts.

ELENA   ooh no. too quiet, everyone tiptoeing around, all those dead people lined up beside each other on the shelves, librarians frowning at you for touching anything, like all those stories are theirs. Apparently I'm not the only person who felt that way, because the library I went into was trashed. People had burned the books right in the middle of the floor—

BERN   idiots. You'd think people would know that we would need those things—

ELENA   People didn't think much in those first few weeks, did they? They thought the power was coming back on. It was all just looting and carnage. *(beat)* The children's section was mostly left alone. And they have encyclopedias for kids, you know. I found out who Eeyore was, and then I found the Pooh books.

BERN   and you read them?

ELENA   I read them. I would rather have been Pooh.

BERN   I think they threw me out because I am too much Pooh… a bear of very little brain.

ELENA   You were—free-spirited.

    BERN starts to laugh.

BERN   is that what they called me?

ELENA   that was then

BERN   oh, Elena, I know my failings. I know what they called me. I didn't think I was doing any harm. I was the grasshopper, singing and dancing while the industrious ants were harvesting and storing for the winter.

ELENA   but didn't the ants relent and share with the grasshopper, once they gave him a good tongue-lashing?

BERN   maybe in the Disney version. I think the original was much grimmer than that. They sent him away. Her. They sent her away to starve.

> ELENA *nods.*

see, my mistake was—I didn't think there was anything after—planes drop out of the sky, lights go out, money becomes nothing more than firestarter… I thought, hell, it's the end of the world, let's party, all bets are off. I didn't think we would—line up behind feudal lords. Be assessed on our usefulness. Be found wanting.

ELENA   Joke's on them.

BERN   I guess.

ELENA   turns out you're more useful than most of those who stayed.

BERN   Who knew all that socializing would pay off. Summers up here were all about visiting—dinners at this house, at that cabin, up squatter's road, across the lake—drinking too much red wine and solving the world's problems. Fat lot of good it did us.

ELENA   You kept us alive. You kept me alive. I would've hung around like a fort Indian until I starved or Laird's goons shot me, the way they did the feral dogs.

BERN   I was pissed. I didn't really want to be in that club anyway. Too *Lord of the Flies.* But I was really pissed that they only wanted "women of child-bearing age." The power goes off and suddenly we're nothing more than breed-mares.

ELENA stirs the stew.

what'd you call it, again?

ELENA   what?

BERN moves to ELENA.

BERN   the stew. The rabbit stew. Bipbapbop something—

ELENA   Pebeepebonbon.

BERN   Pe-bee-pe—

ELENA   Pebeepebonbon. *(laughs)* I don't even know why, that's what we called it when I was a kid.

BERN   is that your language?

ELENA   I don't know. I don't think so. Because in the language, a rabbit is—waaboos—and soup would be—saaboo—waaboosaaboo—

BERN   Waaboosaaboo—

ELENA   Which doesn't sound a lot like pebeepebonbon—

BERN   Waaboosaaboo

ELENA   Pebeepebonbon

The woman have moved together over this. There is a touch, easy, then suddenly awkward.

BERN   Elena.

ELENA   Okay, I think we can eat. Bowls, Bern. And you can put spoons on the table.

> BERN *pauses, wanting to take the moment further.* ELENA *squeezes past her, gets bowls.*

BERN   Elena—

ELENA   Spoons.

> BERN *breaks and gets spoons.* ELENA *serves the stew. They sit.*

Thanks to the Creator for this meal. Thanks to this waaboos for giving himself to us for this meal.

BERN   Meegwetch, waaboos.

ELENA   that's right.

BERN   Meegwetch for the shelter, the fire and for you, Elena, who catches and then cooks the waabit for us.

ELENA   Eat.

> *They eat.*

BERN   wow. I can feel myself getting stronger as I eat.

ELENA   *(nodding)* meat. We need meat, Indians. It's in our blood.

BERN   Do you think they—

ELENA   I try not to think of them, Bern.

BERN   I think of them all the time.

ELENA   me too. I wonder how they are doing. If the canned goods have run out. If anyone has died of botulism, or diarrhea, or strep. *(beat)* Yeah, I think about them. But I try not to.

BERN   *(beat)* I think I'll go a little further tomorrow. Down around the lake there's a few cabins, see what treasures I can find. More tea would be nice. Sugar. Mmmm. Some kind of canned vegetables.

ELENA   Wire. The thinner the better, for snares. Pliers. A hammer. Nails.

BERN   this is starting to sound like a pretty heavy pack. I may have to stay out overnight.

ELENA   I'll package some of this to take with you. Just in case. Which means you can't eat it all now.

BERN   just one more spoon

> *BERN goes to dip her spoon into* ELENA's *bowl,* ELENA *smacks her lightly.*

Be the first time we spent a night apart since—

ELENA   I spent most of my life alone. I'll be fine.

BERN   don't you miss it, Elena?

ELENA   miss what?

BERN   Touch.

> ELENA *reacts.*

Intimacy.

ELENA reacts.

Sex.

ELENA phhff

BERN· really.

ELENA Messy. In every way. Complicated. Nope. I am glad to be done
with it. Made everything that much simpler.

BERN it makes me grouchy. No sex. *(beat)* Maybe that's why you are
kinda Eeyore.

ELENA if you find a rifle, don't forget to look for bullets.

MUKWA GEEZIS

Time passes, moving from Spirit Moon, January, to Bear Moon,
February. Again, the passage of time can be indicated by move-
ment and light.

THE STRANGER

BERN is out foraging, near the monk's place. She stops a couple of times, sensing something. Then continues. Then stops.

BERN   hello? Is there someone there?

She takes out a knife.

come out.

SEAMUS enters, hands held apart. He is young enough, handsome, a bit hungry looking.

SEAMUS   Hi.

BERN   *(beat)* Hi?

SEAMUS   yeah, hi. We used to say it all the time to people when we met them.

BERN   Ha.

SEAMUS no, *hi. (beat)* do you think—you could—*(He motions to the knife.)*—it's not very welcoming—

BERN maybe I'm not very welcoming

SEAMUS tough luck for me, then

    BERN considers him for a moment. Puts the knife away.

thank you.

    BERN shrugs.

glad you trust me

BERN I don't

SEAMUS but

BERN that's about me, not you. You may still be a rapist, or a murderer, you may still want to harm me. And if you do, if you try, I will fight you, but you look kinda hungry and not very strong, and I am not hungry and I am strong. So.

SEAMUS So?

BERN So. I don't want to be the kind of person who can kill someone. And if I have a knife, then I am choosing to use the knife, and that means I have to be ready to kill you. I don't think I am that person.

SEAMUS wow. Did you just think all that right now?

    BERN laughs.

what?

BERN   so what are you doing here?

SEAMUS just found myself here.

BERN   where did you come from?

        SEAMUS *points vaguely.*

really. You have been just wandering since the unplugging.

SEAMUS the unplugging? That's what you call it? An apocalypse destroys half the world, and you call it the unplugging?

        BERN *shrugs.*

BERN   I used to think of it as the earth waking and shaking like some great dog, and all the machines and wires being shaken off like so many fleas. The earthquakes in Haiti and Japan, the disappearance of the Maldives… But that was really negative. The unplugging is more—benign.

SEAMUS benign?

BERN   yeah. Like—mild. Harmless, kind of.

SEAMUS benign.

BERN   how old are you?

SEAMUS old enough

BERN   what are you doing here?

SEAMUS free country

      BERN laughs again.

      why do you keep laughing at me?

BERN you say funny things

SEAMUS I don't think I do

BERN what are you doing here?

SEAMUS same as you, probably. Looking for stuff. Trying to stay alive.

BERN where'd you come from? Yeah, yeah, I know. *(She motions vaguely as he did before.)* But it's been seven or eight moons since the unplugging, you haven't been wandering since then. You've been somewhere, you've been part of some community. And now you are not. How come?

SEAMUS Moons? Is that like months?

BERN yes, my boy, that is like months, give or take. Once upon a time we kept time by the moon.

SEAMUS it was a beautiful moon last night. Full.

BERN *almost* a full moon. Today it is full. Mukwa geezis. Bear moon.

SEAMUS Mug—wah?

BERN Mukwa, it means bear.

SEAMUS in what language?

BERN   in my language. So, you won't tell me where you came from, or what you are doing here. You must have just got here, I haven't seen any sign of you.

SEAMUS   yeah, just got here yesterday, was lucky to find this place up here for the night, made a fire

BERN   where? I didn't smell anything—

SEAMUS   Just up there, nice place, all glass and open

BERN   at the monk's place?

SEAMUS   there was no one there

BERN   no, he's gone

SEAMUS   he was a monk? Cool.

BERN   you didn't—wreck it, did you?

SEAMUS   what difference does it make? He's long gone. He won't miss a few chairs—

BERN   Oh no—

SEAMUS   good thing that floor is stone, or the whole place woulda gone up

BERN   what?

She strides to him, poking him as she speaks.

This is how we got into this situation in the first place, people indiscriminately taking and using and wasting without any thought to the future—

SEAMUS ow, ow, okay stop, I'm kidding—I'm just jerking you around!

> BERN *stops. They are too close.*

BERN You didn't—

SEAMUS What kind of asshole do you think I am? shit, you are strong…
I'm gonna have a bruise there.

BERN I barely touched you.

SEAMUS look, it's coming up already

BERN wow, you must be missing something in your diet

> SEAMUS *laughs.*

SEAMUS yeah, like food.

> BERN *reacts.*

you wouldn't have any?

BERN what?

SEAMUS please. The monk's place is nice, but it's kinda stripped clean.
Like every other place along the way here.

BERN along the way?

> *Beat.*

> *She reaches into her pocket and pulls out a package that she
> unwraps a bit, from which she pulls out a piece of food. She
> hands it to him.*

SEAMUS bites it. Chews.

SEAMUS   wow. Holy shit. That's—what is that? Meat?

BERN   it's moose. A kind of a jerky.

SEAMUS   oh my god. You caught a moose?

BERN   my—friend—shot a moose, yes.

> *SEAMUS finishes the bite.*

SEAMUS   is there—more?

> *She pulls out another piece, holds it to him, then away.*

BERN   what are you doing here?

SEAMUS   let's just say I am looking for a new situation

> *He reaches for the jerky. She pulls it away.*

BERN   what was wrong with the old situation?

SEAMUS   please. It's so—good—I'm hungry

> *BERN holds the food away.*

I was in a place, a group of people. They—didn't want me. I wasn't pulling my weight.

> *BERN gives him the meat, which he tries not to wolf down. She reaches into another pocket and offers him something.*

BERN   These are full of vitamin C. Should help with the bruising.

SEAMUS Thank you.

> *BERN nods.*

BERN let me see. *(motions to where she poked him)*

> *He opens his layers and she looks at his chest.*

yup, that's a bruise all right. Sorry.

SEAMUS you smell good.

BERN *(stepping away)* what?

SEAMUS sorry, don't—it's just, you smell good, like woodsmoke and pine trees and vanilla and stars—

BERN I smell like stars?

SEAMUS yeah, I don't know. But yeah, like stars.

> *BERN laughs.*

there you go again.

BERN you're a funny boy—

SEAMUS Seamus

BERN SHAYmuss.

SEAMUS yeah, but spelled the Irish way—s-e-a-m-u-s—my folks had a thing for the old country—though they were born and bred here

BERN   the old country

SEAMUS   people are funny about roots

BERN   yeah

SEAMUS   so—um—

BERN   um?

SEAMUS   that's your opening to say—my name is—Cathy or Stephanie
           or Michelle or whatever

BERN   I don't know that I want to give you my name.

SEAMUS   o-kay. Well, then I will just call you She Who Smells Like
           Stars. Though it's a little awkward. Better hope there's no
           emergency. Watch out! She Who Smells Like Stars! There's
           a—awwwwww!
           And the bear will have you.

BERN   no bears out this time of year.

SEAMUS   even though it's bear moon? Mugwah something.

BERN   good for you, Seamus. You learned something.

SEAMUS   I can learn things. I can. It's a bit late, but—

BERN   Bernadette.

SEAMUS   Bernadette.

BERN   but my friends—my friend—calls me Bern.

SEAMUS   ah, your friend. Am I going to meet her?

BERN   how do you know it's a her?

SEAMUS   you said, your friend, she shot a moose

BERN   I don't think I did

SEAMUS   well, even if you didn't, don't take this the wrong way, She Who Smells Like Stars, but you don't seem like a woman who has a man

> *BERN nods.*

do you wanna go up to the monk's house, make a fire? Then you can see for yourself that I didn't bust up the joint.

> *BERN pauses.*

come on, Bernadette. And if you have any more of that jerky in those pockets, I'll trade you news for a piece of it.

> *He starts to walk off, beckoning her. After a moment she follows him.*

CACHE

BERN is doing housework. ELENA bursts through the door carrying the hatchet. She gets the rifle, starts to load it.

BERN   Elena, what—?

ELENA   they've found us

BERN   who's found us? Wait, Elena—

ELENA   not now, Bernadette.

BERN grabs the rifle barrel, ELENA still holds the stock.

BERN   what—are—you—doing?

ELENA   there's a man out there. Watching us.

BERN   a man?

ELENA   they've sent someone, Bernadette. They tracked us, and they've sent someone—

BERN   why would they do that, Elena?

ELENA   to take what we have. Let go.

BERN   you're not going to shoot him

ELENA   I am going to try.

BERN   he's hardly a man, Elena. Not much more than a boy.

> *ELENA stops. Beat. Beat.*

I met him. Yesterday. Up near the monk's place.

ELENA   you—*met*—him?

BERN   yeah, I was on my way back from the creek and I could feel that I was being watched. So I called him out.

ELENA   you met him yesterday? And you didn't tell me?

BERN   I'm sorry, Elena. I was trying to figure out how to—tell you.

> *ELENA is silent.*

I was afraid. Of this. That you would take a gun to him.

ELENA   you met him yesterday.

BERN   I'm sorry. *(beat)* Elena, can we invite him in?

ELENA   no.

BERN   no?

ELENA   absolutely not.

BERN   I don't get a say in this?

ELENA   how about, I don't get a say in this. You go off and meet some
         man, you don't tell me, now you want to bring him into our
         house.

BERN   sorry, sorry, sorry, how many times can I say it? I'm sorry. Elena,
         it's cold out there, he is hungry. He's young, and kinda dumb.

ELENA   Send him back to them. Tell them no.

BERN   They banished him.

ELENA   *(beat)* Sure they did.

BERN   That's what he says.

ELENA   Don't believe him, Bernadette. He's a man.

BERN   oh my god

ELENA   How long did you two stand around chatting? Or was it more
         than chatting?

BERN   It was more like talking, Elena. Not too long. Long enough.
         He's staying in the monk's place.

ELENA   nooooo

BERN   no, it's okay. I checked. He is being respectful. Showed him
         how to make a proper fire.

ELENA   you were in the monk's place with him

BERN   He has news, Elena, lots of news. Just let him come in, have a cup of tea, something to eat. He can tell you things. He has news. Maybe about your daughter, your grandson.

ELENA   they are dead to me

BERN   they are not dead to you, Elena. Even if they are dead *(She makes a physical gesture to banish the thought.)* they would still not be dead to you. "They are with us, always." *(beat)* Let me invite him in.

ELENA   do you like him?

BERN   oh, Elena. He's a boy, he's like a nephew.

> *Big beat.* ELENA *looks at* BERN, *weighing.* BERN *waits.*

ELENA   all right. Let's see him then.

> BERN *goes to the door.*

BERN   Seamus!

ELENA   Seamus?

SEAMUS   *(offstage)* Bern?

BERN   Come on in! *(to* ELENA*)* You might want to put the rifle down.

ELENA   or, I might not.

> SEAMUS *arrives at the door. He comes in, taking off his boots.*

SEAMUS   Hi. You must be Elena.

SEAMUS *tries to offer his hand, considers the gun, changes his mind.*

I have heard so much about you.

ELENA   really. From whom.

SEAMUS   well, from—Bernadette here. *(beat)* Oh hey, Bern, *(reaching in his parka pocket)* are these the same berries you gave me yesterday?

BERN   rose hips. Yeah.

ELENA *raises her eyebrows.*

SEAMUS   oh good. I thought so. I found some more today. Been sucking on them. 'Cause of what you said about vitamin C. Ooh, wanna see the bruise you gave me? *(starts to undo his shirt)* It's a good one.

BERN   ah, that's okay. Um, come on in. Do you want a cup of tea?

ELENA   Bernadette—

SEAMUS   oh please. *(to ELENA)* Thank you for having me in your home.

ELENA *nods.* BERN *motions for him to sit, then brings him a cup of tea.*

meegwitch. That's right, isn't it? Thank you?

BERN   Meegwetch. Yes.

SEAMUS *sees* ELENA *watching him.*

SEAMUS   Bern taught me that. Thank you. In your language.

ELENA   you're a quick learner, are you?

SEAMUS   pretty quick. Things that interest me. Though now there's a lot less distractions, I find that a lot of things interest me. Everything. It's like the—the unplugging—kind of wiped me clean, and I can start learning all over again. But important things this time, not just video games and Twitter, but things like what time of day it is from the sun, and what we can eat from the land, and that mukwa means bear—

ELENA   what are you here for?

SEAMUS   I told Bern—

ELENA   tell me

BERN   Elena

SEAMUS   it's okay, Bern. I know it must look weird, me showing up here. The community—it's not going so well there. *(beat)* There's lots of—sickness, lots of anger, lots of power stuff going on. Laird is, like, king or something. He said I had to go because I wasn't pulling my weight, but I think it was—something else.

BERN   something else?

SEAMUS   I was doing the same as everyone else. More, even, because I was strong, but Laird—nothing I did pleased him.

ELENA   And.

SEAMUS   There was a girl. New since you two—left—I think. Tessera. We were spending time together. And Laird, well, he seems to think that everything and everyone belongs to him.

BERN   droit du seigneur

SEAMUS what?

BERN   it's—nothing—a primitive belief—

ELENA   so she wouldn't leave with you?

SEAMUS Tessera, she's young. She's scared. She's lost a lot—

ELENA   We've all lost a lot.

SEAMUS yeah, well, yeah… I don't blame her. I couldn't have taken care of her. I could barely take care of myself. If I didn't find you guys—

ELENA   so you tracked us here

SEAMUS yeah

ELENA   why?   BERN   how?

ELENA   surely there were other options along the way, other groups of people who would be happy to have a young, able-bodied, quick learner like you

SEAMUS *(shrugs)* maybe. Stayed with a few on the way. Passed a few more. Nothing appealed.

ELENA   and we did? Two old women? What did you think was going to happen when you got here?

SEAMUS I didn't think that far—I don't know. I just kept moving north. *(beat)* Then I stumbled on one of your camps. Saw how you got in, that you'd made a small fire, burned your garbage, left the place tidy. That there were two of you.

ELENA you're a regular detective, are you?

SEAMUS I started to try and think like you. Where were you going, how did you choose your stopping places… you were smart… you made me smarter.

ELENA We made you smarter. So now you think that we should welcome you with open arms?

SEAMUS I didn't think you would welcome me with open arms. It's why I hung around, getting the lay of the land for a bit. But I got—

ELENA —hungry.

SEAMUS —lonely. *(beat)* We need people. People. People need people.

Silence.

BERN how did you find us?

Silence.

how did you find us, Seamus? How did you even know to keep moving north? Elena and I have been gone for three moons. You didn't just walk out on the road and sniff. I never even saw you when we were there.

He looks at ELENA.

SEAMUS I know your daughter, Valerie. We talked. She worries about you.

ELENA   shut up

SEAMUS she—she's pretty busted up—

ELENA   Shut up!

SEAMUS and your grandson, Archer, he said when he saw you again
         he'd—

ELENA   GET OUT! GET OUT!

         ELENA grabs the rifle.

BERN   Elena, NO! *(to SEAMUS)* You'd better go.

         SEAMUS struggles into his boots, exits.

         BERN picks up the abandoned cup, examines it.

         so now we banish him?

ELENA   I don't want to talk about it

BERN   how does that make us different from Laird?

ELENA   I said I don't want to talk about it. *(beat)* I am tired, Bernadette.
         I am going to lie down.

         ELENA exits. BERN lifts the cup to her lips, finishes SEAMUS's tea.

SNOW CRUST MOON

Time passes, moving from Bear Moon, February, to Snow Crust
Moon, March. Again, the passage of time can be indicated by
movement and light.

GENEROSITY

BERN is doing chores.

BERN   "I could drink a case of you—oo oo oo darling—and I would
still be on my feet—oh I would still be on my feet—"

ELENA   what are you doing?

BERN   I'm cleaning—

ELENA   You're singing

BERN   Oh—was I?

ELENA   *(beat)* you— *(taking a shot)* you've been with him

BERN   what?

ELENA   *(confirming)* you were. With him.

BERN   how did you get to that—from me singing?

ELENA   oh, Bernadette.

BERN   oh, Elena.

ELENA goes silent. BERN busies herself doing things.

what difference does it make if I did. It's just sex, Elena.

ELENA   it is never that simple

BERN   ha.

ELENA looks at her.

well, you're right. It turns out that things are both simpler and more complicated. It turns out that sex is just sex, just as they always maintained, the boys, the men, the husbands and lovers. But the absence of it—that's what makes it a thing. Suddenly its not just sex, it's a self-esteem destroyer, a depressant, a nostalgia…

ELENA just looks at her.

Sometimes, I would go downtown, pick up some young fella, buy him a meal, just to talk to him.

ELENA   you did not!

BERN   okay, I did not

ELENA   you did, didn't you?

BERN   I wasn't ready to be asexual, Elena, I wasn't ready to be invisible

ELENA   young men

BERN young men. Not so young men. Businessmen. Businessmen in hotels. Airport hotels. Easy pickins.

ELENA Bernadette

BERN I understand more about men now… that when you say "fuck me" *(as an exclamation, not an invitation)* and their ears prick up and they say "fuck you?" They really mean it in that moment, they do. But you can't go getting all jealous about his wife, or the blond intern who is making cow eyes at him. What he means, what they all mean, in that moment is I will fuck you, if you are offering. I will fuck almost anyone who will let me.

> *ELENA is flustered, starts working at something.*

too much?

ELENA this is not about—that—

BERN that?

ELENA about your life before this. You're a different person now.

BERN am I

ELENA you're not the grasshopper anymore. You're serious, and smart. Clever. You have made us a life here.

BERN Survival is not a life.

ELENA this is a life. We can't know what is going to happen next. We couldn't foresee the unplugging—

BERN well, I could. I did.

ELENA   maybe you did, but you didn't prepare for it. You certainly didn't foresee this life

BERN   no. no, I didn't.

ELENA   we are becoming, Bernadette. Becoming who we are.

BERN   Elena. I don't want to be joyless.

ELENA   sex is not joy

        BERN smiles.

BERN   it kind of is. not necessarily lasting. not happyeverafter, just a quicksilver moment with which we are gifted a few hundred times in our lives.

ELENA   pretty words. you're—you're—you're avoiding—because this is not about that—about sexual congress

BERN   Sexual congress? What century did you just drop in from?

ELENA   that is not what we are talking about here. You didn't just— have sex—with him. You got intimate with him.

BERN   it's hard to do it otherwise

ELENA   I know about sex, Bernadette. I know how it makes you feel. That it's the last card in the deck, and once you do it, you think you know all about the other. You think you know him.

BERN   that's what I am trying to tell you, Elena, it's not such a big deal. It is, and it isn't. *(beat)* I'm not going to love you any less, Elena.

ELENA   what are you talking about?

BERN   he's not a threat

ELENA   of course he's a threat, Bernadette. He is a threat to everything
we have built here. You are jeopardizing everything we have.

BERN   he's not a threat to you and me

ELENA   how can you—be intimate—with him, when he comes from
them. They banished us, Bernadette, they sent us off without so
much as a can of food. Now they are starving, we have plenty,
and they want what we have.

BERN   all right, you win. Sex is never that simple.

ELENA   he hasn't come back to take us, just to take what we know.

BERN   how can I not teach him? We are surrounded by food.

ELENA   let him starve

ABANDON

In the darkness the sound of lovemaking, ending with orgasm.
Lights up on BERN *and* SEAMUS, *post-coital.*

SEAMUS were you always so—

BERN libidinous?

SEAMUS I was going to say horny.

BERN of course you were.

SEAMUS *(trying it on)* libidinous. Libidinous. It sounds—slinky. I like it.
So?

BERN no. I was kind of judgmental and inflexible when I was young-
er. I wish I had known. I would've had a lot more sex and a
lot less angst.

SEAMUS well you're pretty flexible now

BERN funny

SEAMUS   hey, do you have anything to eat?

BERN   oh sorry, yeah, I brought you meat

> *She digs in her parka and finds a package, gives it to him. He eats ravenously, trying not to appear starving.*

I'm sorry it's not more. Elena is watching the supplies really closely. Now that she knows.

SEAMUS   s'okay. You're not my mom. *(beat)* Bern? I was thinking, I've gotta move on.

BERN   what? why? No.

SEAMUS   I can't stay like this. I am not pulling my weight. Again.

BERN   listen it's only a matter of time before Elena gets over—

SEAMUS   You're taking care of me. You barely have enough for you two and here I am sharing your food—

BERN   we have lots, Seamus, the moose will get all of us through the winter, there's still some cabins up the road that are sure to have more canned stuff. Elena is a good hunter, and she's taught me how to preserve (meat)—

> *She stops suddenly, wondering if she is saying too much.*

SEAMUS   what

BERN   nothing

SEAMUS   *(He hears her suspicion.)* ah. *(beat)* I'll go tomorrow.

BERN   where will you go?

SEAMUS I don't know. I honest to god don't have a clue. Can't go back. Everything else is just unknown. But I can't stay here, like a pet, being fed once in a while, stroked once in a while, waiting for the sound of your boots. It's pathetic. I am pathetic.

BERN   it's hard. These are hard times. We are all having to—become—something new. What did you do before this?

SEAMUS I was a bike courier.

BERN   a bike courier.

SEAMUS yeah. Crazy now, to think of it. What an absolutely useless job. Not one skill I can use in this brave new world. Never made a single thing that mattered. Never made a thing that would tell the world that I had existed. Moving envelopes from here to there, without a clue what was in them, not caring. Not caring.

BERN   That explains these muscular legs... and your stamina.

SEAMUS Probably had a lot to do with my survival. The city was nuts—chaos. I got on my bike and pedalled north.

BERN   did you want to be something? Something else?

SEAMUS *(beat)* I should make something up, eh? Make myself sound better or smarter or more interesting. But. No. not really. I was a grasshopper too. Ride around all day, drink beer with my friends, flirt with the girls. Never save a penny. Never learn a thing. Never even wonder where my ambition was. It was all fun, it all seemed full, and busy. It seemed like a life. But looking back on it now. Wow.

BERN   I can teach you.

SEAMUS   teach me what?

BERN   how to catch your own food.

SEAMUS   a moose?

BERN   no. I don't know how to do that. I haven't done it yet any-
            way. But Elena taught me to catch rabbit. So I can teach you
            to catch rabbit. And I can show you willow, and how to find
            water, and what is edible even though it's Snow Crust Moon.

SEAMUS   what will Elena say?

BERN   she'll be mad. But I think it's wrong to hoard

PINK MOON

BERN is sitting stoney in the cabin. ELENA bustles in.

ELENA   Bern! Look! Look at this, do you know what this is?

BERN   not a clue.

ELENA   what's wrong with you? Look, this was growing. Growing. Oh my, there is going to be fresh food soon, fresh green things. We can start to plant soon, we'll know soon what wintered over—what is wrong with you?

BERN   Seamus is gone.

ELENA   gone? Gone where?

BERN   I don't know. Just gone.

ELENA   just gone? Like, gone he met a spring bear and lost?

BERN   nice.

ELENA   some days you get the bear, some days the bear gets you

BERN   gone on purpose. His stuff is gone.

ELENA   damn.

BERN   what do you care?

ELENA   where do you think he has gone, Bernadette? Now that you
have taught him everything you know, everything I taught you.
He's gone back, bearing that gift, to that place, that place that
spat us out like rotten meat. It is his passport back in.

BERN   So what if he did, Elena. They need to know. Maybe they will
let him back in, and if he wants to be there, then good, I am
glad I was able to help him get back in. It wasn't ours to keep

ELENA   he wasn't, you mean.

BERN   not him, Elena. He—he was sweet and distracting—but he
didn't take anything from me that I didn't want to give. No, I
mean the knowledge, the things I taught him, the things you
taught me, maybe he will go back and teach your daughter

>   ELENA *sucks her teeth.*

and isn't that the way it is supposed to be? Isn't that the thing
we were bemoaning just before the lights went out? That no
one knew where their food came from, that our men refused
to take responsibility for anything?

ELENA   How is this taking responsibility?

BERN   if he has gone back to teach them—

ELENA   teach them? How long before they show up here with weapons to take it by force?

BERN   he wouldn't do that—

ELENA   he stalked us, hunted us and stole from us

BERN   he didn't steal—

ELENA   Really? He left with just the clothes on his back?

> BERN *suddenly pales, exits in a hurry.*

SUCKER MOON

Time passes, moving from Pink Moon, April, to Sucker Moon, May. Again, the passage of time can be indicated by movement and light.

HARVEST

BERN is doing chores.

ELENA calls from outside, distressed.

ELENA   Bern! Bern!

BERN grabs the gun, checking it as she goes to the door.

When she throws it open, ELENA is standing there with a fish.

BERN   Jesus, Elena, you scared the hell out of me. I thought a bear—

ELENA   what is this?

BERN   I'm not so good on fish yet, Elena. A—trout?

ELENA   what is it doing here?

BERN   here?

ELENA   here. On the step.

*ELENA enters, putting the fish on the counter. BERN closes the
door behind her.*

What is a fresh fish doing here on the step?

BERN   the fish was on the step?

ELENA   you didn't do this? As some kind of a joke?

BERN   be a pretty dumb joke. Lucky a bear didn't come sniffing
around

ELENA   well it didn't crawl the mile up the hill from the lake, and it
didn't fall out of the sky

BERN   maybe the bear brought it

ELENA   Bern. Focus. Someone left it on our doorstep.

BERN   an offering of some kind

ELENA   an offering

BERN   from someone who wants to know us. Or thinks he owes us.
Someone who stole from us. Someone who took food from
us and slipped away.

She goes to the door, opens it.

Seamus?

ELENA   Seamus?

SEAMUS appears in the doorway.

SEAMUS Hi.

BERN Hi?

SEAMUS Yeah, hi. We used to say it all the time to people when we met them. *(beat)* Do you think—you could—*(He motions to the gun.)*—it's not very welcoming—

BERN maybe I'm not very welcoming

SEAMUS you got my peace offering. *(beat)* I caught it myself.

> *Beat.*

ELENA have you eaten?

> *She lifts the fish, smells it.*

fresh. *(beat)* Good for you. Do you know how to clean it?

SEAMUS I *have* done it. I *can* do it.

ELENA that doesn't sound too promising. I'll do it, and then we will have fresh fish for breakfast.

> *ELENA exits with the fish.*

> *A pause.*

SEAMUS Bern.

> *He moves towards her, she lifts the gun.*

BERN don't bother

SEAMUS   oh. So you have decided that this *is* the kind of person you are? the kind of person who can kill someone?

     BERN lowers the gun.

BERN   no. I guess not.

     BERN puts the gun away.

SEAMUS   I would like to explain.

BERN   you stole from us. I trusted you, I showed you how to survive, and then you stole food, you took snares, and matches, and—

SEAMUS   I'm sorry. I had to go back. I needed supplies. I only took what I needed. I learned that from you, Bern.

BERN   so Elena was right all along. She was wiser than me, she told me, you were only here to take what we knew.

SEAMUS   she was wiser, but you were more generous. And that— changed everything.

     ELENA enters with the cleaned fish and greens.

ELENA   it's a beautiful fish, Seamus. I cleaned it at the creek, so its guts can go back to the water. Chi meegwetch.

BERN   What is going on here? He steals from us, he uses it to get back in to that place and you are treating him like the prodigal son. Why are you back here, Seamus? What else can you take from us?

ELENA   He didn't take it, Bern. You gave it. Freely. You told me that.

BERN   so this is just a friendly visit then

SEAMUS   friendly, yes. Just, no. Not just a friendly visit. More of a diplomatic mission, really.

BERN   really.

ELENA   the community wants something from us

      SEAMUS nods.

BERN   you were right, Elena, you were right about everything. I'm an idiot, a blind, pathetic idiot—

ELENA   hush.

BERN   hush?

ELENA   what did they send you for this time, Seamus? What do they want?

BERN   'Cause the moose is all gone. Had to finish it before the thaw. There's a couple of jars of the potted stuff left—

ELENA   Bernadette.

BERN   are they out there? Waiting with guns? Waiting for a signal?

ELENA   he brought a fish, Bernadette, not a gun

BERN   maybe it's a Trojan fish

SEAMUS   they are out there. A few of them, and they are waiting for a signal from me.

The women react.

To come in and talk. To make reparations. To ask you to come back to the community.

ELENA to come back?

SEAMUS You were right, Elena. I was sent, back in mukwa geezis, to find out how you were doing. I thought I would take whatever you had, take it back—the community was in such bad shape. And then I got here, and you had plenty, and you shared.

ELENA well, Bernadette did.

BERN I only had anything because you shared with me

SEAMUS and I stayed because I realized that if I learned, that would be way more useful to the village than just a side of moose

ELENA teach a man to fish

SEAMUS or to snare waaboos. But as I learned to fish, I couldn't help but learn other things too, and compare this life, the life you were building, with the life back in the village. I wanted to stay. I did. But.

ELENA but you had a mission

SEAMUS when I got back, things were worse. Laird wanted to raid you, take everything. I told him I wouldn't bring him here. He couldn't have done it anyway. He was sick, lots of the villagers were, people were dying. The ones who were healthy, we started to trap, to work for the village. Making soup, working in teams. People started getting better. Some didn't. Laird didn't.

We nursed him—to death. When he died, we started to talk about new leaders. And—elder—leaders.

ELENA I don't want to go back.

BERN tell them thank you, nice story.

SEAMUS the village needs you, Elena.

> BERN *snorts.*

we need both of you.

I realize you have no reason to trust us, to trust me. But maybe if we can just sit, and talk, about possible futures.

ELENA do you want your people to come in, Seamus? Have a cup of tea?

BERN Elena!

SEAMUS I think they would like that. But Elena. you should know. There are three of them. Will, he's a good man, handy, brave. And a woman and a boy. She won't come in if you don't want to see her. But the boy, Archer, he wouldn't let me come without him. He says you have something of his.

ELENA Valerie is out there

> BERN *moves to* ELENA.

BERN are you all right?

ELENA I'm fine.

BERN   are you sure?

ELENA   oh, Bernadette. You were right. You were right.

BERN   about what? I feel like I have been absolutely wrong about every single thing every step of the way—

ELENA   oh my

BERN   what?

ELENA   they must be hungry. Throw a couple of sticks on the fire, Bern, and the pan. Cut up those onions there, and maybe some garlic—

> ELENA *starts preparing for company.* BERN *does as she is told.*

we are going to have to set up a summer kitchen soon, Bern, so we don't have to heat the house just to cook.

BERN   uh huh

SEAMUS   what's a summer kitchen?

BERN   I dunno. But I'm sure I'll find out. *(pause)* And then you will.

SEAMUS   you're a good teacher

BERN   *(pause)* you were a good student

SEAMUS   I can be again.

ELENA   Seamus. You can call them in.

She comes to the door, fussing a bit about her appearance. SEAMUS
stands with his hand on the door.

They wait. They still wait.

SEAMUS Wait, just a moment. I want to remember—everything.

They wait.

Blackout.

ACKNOWLEDGEMENTS

Many individuals and the organizations they represent have contributed to the development of this play: Donna-Michelle St. Bernard and Native Earth Performing Arts, Maureen Labonté and the Banff Playwrights Colony, Rachel Ditor and Bill Millerd and the Arts Club Theatre, Heidi Taylor and Martin Kinch and the Playwrights Theatre Centre.

In addition, I would like to acknowledge Velma Wallis and her retelling of the Athabaskan story *Two Old Women*, Liz Frankel at the Public Theater for her ongoing support, DD Kugler, Randy Reinholz and Philip Adams.

Yvette Nolan is a playwright, dramaturg and director. She has written several plays, including *Annie Mae's Movement*, *BLADE* and *Job's Wife*. She has been writer-in-residence at Brandon University, Mount Royal College and the Saskatoon Public Library, as well as playwright-in-residence at the National Arts Centre. Born in Saskatchewan to an Algonquin mother and an Irish immigrant father and raised in Manitoba, Yvette lived in the Yukon and Nova Scotia before moving to Toronto where she served as Artistic Director of Native Earth Performing Arts from 2003 to 2011.